GW00854903

THE
FUNNIEST
QPR
QUOTES...
EVER!

Copyright © 2018 by Gordon Law

No part of this publication may be reproduced, stored in a retrieval system or transmitted in any form by any means, electronic, mechanical, photocopying, or otherwise, without prior written permission of the publisher Gordon Law.

gordonlawauthor@yahoo.com

Printed in Europe and the USA

ISBN: 9781729335178
Imprint: Independently published

Photos courtesy of: Ramzi Musallam

Contents

Introduction

"I couldn't be more chuffed if I were a badger at the start of the mating season" was one of the funniest one-liners from Ian Holloway.

As QPR player and manager, Holloway not only delivered on the pitch but off it as well with a vast array of brilliant sound bites when speaking to the media.

His most memorable was probably the time he compared a scrappy win over Chesterfield to taking an ugly girl home in a taxi in what was a bizarre post-match analogy.

He once bemoaned his luck by saying, "If I fell in a barrel of boobs I'd come out sucking my thumb" and after leading Rangers to promotion said, "Every dog has his day, and today is 'Woof Day'. Today, I just want to bark!"

Holloway is not the only colourful character to have taken the Rangers hot seat with Harry Redknapp loving a comic remark as much as an entertaining anecdote, while Neil Warnock had us chuckling with his honest observations and rants at referees.

In the boardroom, there have been some cracking quips from Flavio Briatore and Tony Fernandes, popcorn moments from midfielder Joey Barton's verbal bashings on Twitter and Stan Bowles' tales of off-field antics have been highly amusing.

Their classic lines and many more can be found in this unique collection of quotations and I hope you laugh as much reading this book as I did in compiling it.

Gordon Law

THE FUNNIEST QPR QUOTES... EVER!

CAN YOU MANAGE?

"I'm sick and tired of every Tom, Dick and Harry getting linked with my job every day. Well ding, dang, do. It's my job, I own it and it's up to anyone else to take it off me."

Ian Holloway under pressure as QPR boss

"The club has galloped forward and I want to try and bring it back a little bit. If we are a horse, we are not a race horse, we are a horse that is going to try and pull a cart and make sure everybody is on it. I don't want to gallop off and look all lovely with shiny shoes on saying 'look at me'. That's not what we are. We are an old cob of a fella that is going to drag everybody with us."

Ian Holloway on his return as QPR manager

"They must know somebody at the Football League, Norwich, getting their fixtures like they have. Poor old Dave Jones [former Cardiff City manager] was moaning about it the other day, I think Delia Smith must be cooking something for them."

Neil Warnock reckons the Canaries have a favourable Championship run-in

"The days of walking in, shouting and screaming and throwing teacups at players were gone. There is no point effing and blinding at a player who can hardly speak English."

Harry Redknapp is a much calmer manager these days

"When Crouch was first mentioned, I didn't think we could afford one of his shoe laces."

Neil Warnock says Tottenham striker Peter Crouch is out of QPR's price range

"We've got to be solid and horrible to break down, I don't want to be southern softies!"

Ian Holloway on QPR's tougher attitude

"I tell my children they must have good manners. I'm okay except between five to three and 10 to five during a game. Then somebody else takes over."

Neil Warnock becomes his alter ego when he is in the dugout

"This place hasn't changed since I was here as a player 21 years ago. The wallpaper is still the same in Tel's old office. It's got the same desk, the same leather chair he used. His wallet's not there, though!"

John Gregory on the Terry Venables remnants

"I've had a week from hell, I'm trying to learn how to relax. I'm now going to enjoy this, take my brain out and stick it in an ice bucket."

Ian Holloway can chill out after QPR's win

"There are no mountains in Wolverhampton."

Stewart Houston when asked if his side "had a mountain to climb" ahead of a tie at Wolves

"Twenty minutes from kick-off, with the lads about to come in from their warm-up, I was in the dressing room getting my thoughts ready when my phone went. I thought it must be someone important to ring me at this time. I answered and a guy said, 'Mr Warnock? It's Specsavers here. Your contact lenses have arrived, will you be picking them up?'"

Neil Warnock did go to Specsavers!

"I took them orienteering on Monday – and two of them got lost. We had to go out in a van to get them. I can't tell you who they are because they are a little embarrassed."

Ian Holloway on a pre-season trip to Scotland

"Most of our fans get behind us and are fantastic but those who don't should shut the hell up or they can come round to my house and I will fight them."
Ian Holloway's ultimatum to the supporters

"I'm not allowed to speak to Joe. Are you trying to get me banned by the FA or something?!"
Harry Redknapp when asked if he has spoken to Joe Cole about signing for QPR

"If we did get in the play-offs, I'd be singing and dancing but it would be a horrible song as I can't sing a note!"
Ian Holloway – honest as the day is long

"We did have time for some sight-seeing, wandering round the square and through the souks. We saw all the snake-charmers with their cobras. I was a bit disappointed no one offered to swap [my wife] Sharon for a camel."

Neil Warnock on a scouting trip to Morocco

"Joe Royle texted me to say keeping us up would be like – was it turning fish into something, or water into wine, or feeding the 5,000? I've never read the Bible but I think he meant it would be a miracle."

Harry Redknapp after joining QPR in 2012... they ended up relegated

"In football, there is no definite lifespan or time span for a manager. After a while you start smelling of fish. The other week it looked like I was stinking of Halibut!"

Ian Holloway on the very fickle nature of management after Rangers' poor start

"I am not a pair of bell bottoms. I am not a high waisted pair you had at school with the pockets so big you could get your books in. I'm not that pair of trousers. I'm getting re-tailored all the time to get in fashion because that is what you have to do, because the game is changing all the time."

Ian Holloway feels he has evolved as a manager on his return to QPR

"I had a one-night stand with a new bedtime partner this week. There are pictures too, but there is no need to get a super-injunction to keep it quiet. Sharon knew and she was very understanding. After we won the Championship on Monday I took the trophy home... So that night I asked Sharon, did she mind if I slept with it? I love her to bits, but it was only for one night. She slept in the spare room."
Neil Warnock slept with the original Football League trophy after QPR won the title

"We are not instant coffee here – this is long term and I want to help lift our brand even higher."
Ian Holloway after signing a new contract

Can You Manage?

"I am a football manager. I can't see into the future. Last year I thought I was going to Cornwall on my holidays but I ended up going to Lyme Regis!"

Ian Holloway on whether his QPR team could beat Manchester City

"[My wife] Sharon was a wreck, crying her eyes out. I thought at first she was re-watching the last episode of Downton Abbey."

Neil Warnock after getting sacked by QPR

"I love to be around people who are prepared to kick their granny."

John Gregory likes physical players

"It is completely dead out there. I've been phoning myself up and disguising my voice just for a bit of interest."

Manager Gerry Francis on QPR's lack of action in the transfer window

"If I was the invisible man for a day, I'd hang around the QPR dressing room to hear what the players say about me."

Harry Redknapp on his ideal superpower

"You have to ask about a bar of soap at this club. I even had to pay for our pre-match meal on my own credit card on Saturday."

Ian Holloway on QPR's financial constraints

"I'll always fight my corner, say what I want. Sometimes it gets you in trouble but that's what Yorkshire people are like."

Neil Warnock is honest as ever

"I've got to get Dan Shittu ready for the Stoke game. I've told him to go to Iceland and ask if he can sit in one of their freezers."

Ian Holloway wasn't sure if there were enough ice packs for his giant defender

"I am off to Cornwall to get on my tractor for a few days."

Neil Warnock will plough some fields after getting fired

"Hopefully he [Malky Mackay] will learn from what he has done but everyone does the tweeting and texting. I don't send text messages, but I do receive them with sick jokes. I don't read them, they make me ill."

Harry Redknapp's not much of a texter

"Our promotion has brought a few journos out of the woodwork who seem to have a grudge against me, particularly Patrick Collins in The Mail on Sunday. I take Collins' columns to bed with me, I suffer from insomnia and find after a couple of his paragraphs I drop off for a good night's sleep."

Neil Warnock is not happy with the writer's article on him

"It's like when I was a kid waiting for Santa to turn up, worried whether I'd been good enough. To then see he has and he's given you a few toys – this is even better than that feeling. That excitement and exhilaration when you open the door and can see the presents – this is even better than that."

Ian Holloway on the joys of promotion

"I think Paul [Lambert] was embarrassed when he accepted it, to be honest. There was only one Manager of the Year in my eyes."

Neil Warnock after the Norwich boss claimed the award, despite Warnock's Championship title win with QPR

"Who will Sky have to interview through a car window if I am not here on transfer deadline day?"

A light-hearted Harry Redknapp does not fear losing his QPR job

"A load of old b*llocks."

Redknapp on suggestions he is on the verge of the sack at the 19th-placed side

"I'm not a communicator by tweet, I'm afraid, so I was always going to be the last to know."

Neil Warnock after being sacked by QPR whose owner Tony Fernandes loved to tweet

"We did a scam television programme. This fella was brought into training, allegedly called Eduardo and Latvia's captain. We told the players a rich guy had just bought the club and wanted him in his team. He was cack, absolutely useless. But I said it was out of my hands and they had to give him a chance. And they fell for it. After 10 minutes of training the lads were booting him up in the air. It was really funny."

Ian Holloway brought in a fake player to a QPR training session as a practical joke

"I'm a people person and I can't wait to work with these people."

New boss Ian Holloway, a man of the people

BOARDROOM BANTER

"When you shook hands with him, you counted your fingers."

Tommy Docherty on his former QPR chairman Jim Gregory

"If you've met a lovely women, do you really worry about what she did before she met you?"

Chairman Gianni Paladini on Luigi de Canio, who has managed many clubs

"If I am taking someone else's money, then I am going to work bloody hard for that person."

Chairman Tony Fernandes is fed up with the attitude of the players

"I can confirm we will not be erecting crosses on the side of the stadium or holding mass weddings on the Loftus Road pitch."

Hoops executive David Davies on reports QPR were getting taken over by the Unification Church

"I don't necessarily think I have to be an a*shole to be successful in football. I think I have to be smarter than I have been and experience is something that you can't buy. Nobody can train you for relegation, nobody can train you for a player who refuses to play because he is a substitute. You learn."

Tony Fernandes is picking things up quickly as a club owner

"I believe Mr Kinnear, who I have never met in my life, has got a heart condition so the last thing I suggest to him is get involved with a club like QPR – he will be dead before he even starts."

Chairman Gianni Paladini tells Joe Kinnear Loftus Road is not an option for him

"He loves you or he hates you. When he loves you, there is no better company in the world You can talk about Gianni being a waiter. You can talk about Gianni being Italian. You can talk about Gianni being an agent. But Gianni is a bloke. Gianni is a fella. A nice fella."

Ian Holloway on Gianni Paladini

"In a fairly dull kingdom, there were two players who were perfectly happy because they had firm contracts. However, due to a shortage of beans, the two players were dispatched to far-flung kingdoms to ply their trade with other clubs."

Chairman David Davies pens some bizarre programme notes

"Tony, can I ring you back? I'm just doing an interview, mate you've ruined it. I'm fined now. I'm fined. I'm fined. Alright mate, I'll ring you back. Thanks."

Ian Holloway takes a call from boss Tony Fernandes and breaks a club rule for allowing a phone to ring during interviews

"When someone arrives in a new business, everybody says this is the new blood to suck. There is nothing to suck here. We don't have blood."

Chairman Flavio Briatore won't led the club bleed him dry

Gianni Paladini: "You f*cking b*stard, I am going to kill you, you f*cking b*stard... where are you, f*cking hell where are you?"

Ian Holloway: "I am on the toilet. My wife is in the house. Ask her."

Paladini: "She could be at f*cking Wolves with you."

The QPR chief calls a virus-hit Ian Holloway after believing reports he was to join Wolves

"When I do go to football, I leave at half-time. By then you can see which way it's going. And they close the roads and all that business. I don't want to be delayed for an hour afterwards. I don't stay to have a drink with other directors. I've got nothing to say to them. I don't know what they are talking about. Actually if you ask me to name five of our team, I couldn't. There is that guy who scores goals for us – Taarabt. Routledge I've heard of. They're all bloody nice guys, but I don't mix with them so I don't know them well."

Joint owner Bernie Ecclestone admits he's not a massive fan of the beautiful game

"Each morning I only expect to wake up and shave. The rest I don't know because life is so fragile. Life, for me, is the moment. That's why I don't buy green bananas – who knows what will happen tomorrow? But now that I am with QPR it is amazing."

Flavio Briatore goes bananas

"Mum and dad are splitting up. I don't want them to stay together for our sake because that never works. I feel like the nanny, telling the kids everything is going to be all right."

Ian Holloway on the rows in QPR's boardroom

"If you'd put Schumacher in a Minardi it would have gone nowhere. If you put Kaka in this club it would go nowhere. It is completely mad."
Flavio Briatore, who is also Renault F1 chief

"It's like when you fancy a young lady – we're at the stage where we haven't even started chatting her up yet, let alone buying her a drink."
Chairman Chris Wright on reports about a merger with Wimbledon

"I pay the tip. They take care of the rest."
Flavio Briatore on who stumps up for dinner when he's with QPR's wealthier owners

"This is a terrible injustice. We'll fight to clear Jude's name."

Chairman Bill Power is backing QPR mascot Jude the Cat who was 'sent off' against Preston because officials were confusing him with the players. "How can I be mistaken for a player? I'm a 7ft black cat!" added Jude

"I assume I will die somehow in the club. I am not sure whether my ashes will be thrown around the ground or embalmed at Loftus Road..."

Tony Fernandes jokes that he's going to snuff it at Rangers

"Flavio will be the one wearing the big tie."

Bernie Ecclestone is happy to be the deputy to Flavio Briatore at QPR

"I was still thinking about food. I thought maybe QPR was a barbecue restaurant."

Flavio Briatore was interested in buying a pizzeria before he got the call from QPR

"I don't really want to see the owners have their pants taken down like they have in the past."

Harry Redknapp is keeping tabs on the Hoops wage bill

THE FUNNIEST QPR QUOTES... EVER!

REF
JUSTICE

"My boys deserve better than that. Traore's penalty? Come on! I've never seen anything like that. Traore blows on him! The referee just wants to give a penalty. It's wrong. Not one Aston Villa supporter appealed for a penalty. Then Hutton deliberately handballs it. For the second one, we're told that if you raise your hands, it's a handball and he's raised his hands. But the first one is embarrassing. How can that not be given a penalty? He can't even say he's in a bad position. I felt an injustice. I felt really bad for the lads. But we have great spirit and to do what we did with 10 men was absolutely fabulous. I spoke to the referee afterwards. When you're a young referee, you listen and learn. I think I made some good points."

Neil Warnock slams Michael Oliver

"I have never seen such a stonewall penalty kick in all my life. Even my wife in St Albans could see that it was a penalty."

Ian Holloway on the match against Grimsby

"He offended me, he offended the fans and he offended my players."

Luigi De Canio was offended by the ref after defeat to West Brom

"When their man was sent off, it seemed to wake up the crowd and give them someone to get their teeth into and fortunately for us that was the referee."

Ian Holloway after QPR beat Leicester

"We've got Mike Riley, I've never been a big fan of his refereeing abilities. I've always thought Mike's done well on limited ability to get where he's got. He's what I call a robot referee and now he's in charge of our referees!"

Neil Warnock slams the general manager of the Professional Game Match Officials

"It was lucky that the linesman wasn't stood in front of me as I would have poked him with a stick to make sure he was awake. I only hope he has woken up in time for his drive home this evening."

Ian Holloway isn't impressed with the assistant referee after a QPR loss at Bristol City

"No-one ever fights for the right thing. We're in Brexit now. None of us knew we had to pay however many million or billion to get out of it, did we? They never gave us that information, so we're out of it now. These referees should have that top man who can't run anymore talking to that very good young referee saying, 'Actually that's not a penalty'. I keep saying, let's make sure we get respect. Retire the people that can't run as fast anymore and sit them with a monitor and let them talk to the referee."

Ian Holloway compares the refereeing system to Brexit in a bizarre rant after QPR's draw with Bristol City

"In Italy referees are all handsome, athletic, telegenic. Here they have tubby bellies and they blow up very little because they are not mad about getting noticed."

Flavio Briatore's view on the men in black

"He was consistent right from the first minute to the last."

An ironic Neil Warnock on Lee Probert's display against Swansea

"What the hell the referee saw I don't know – he ought to go to Specsavers."

Ian Holloway slams Lee Probert who awarded a last-minute penalty to Sheffield United

"Certain decisions were ridiculous. It was like the Wild Wild West out there."

Jimmy Floyd Hasselbaink fumes at referee Darren Bond's decisions over Barnsley's second and third goals

"The refereeing was very one-sided but I will take my medicine. I got incensed and said one or two swear words I'm not allowed to say. It's ironic you can get sworn at and intimidated all day and if you show emotion you're in trouble. I'm pleading guilty and I have apologised to the referee. But football is about passion and the day I don't care is the day I give up."

Ian Holloway on the officiating for QPR's draw against Cardiff

"[Josh] Scowen should have been sent off, it's an absolutely scandalous tackle in my opinion. I'm going to hammer him. He got angry because they were playing around us. Well you've got to take your medicine son, don't kick out at someone like that."

Ian Holloway blasts a tackle... by his own player after a 4-0 defeat at Hull City

"F------ EPL refs are a big load of b-------! Biased and blind. Thank you for spoiling the game."

Director Ruben Emir Gnanalingam tweeted after Joey Barton's red card against Norwich, before removing the message

"I asked the linesman how did he not see the penalty. Ridgewell's hand was up there, it's the most blatant handball and he couldn't see it. The linesman said it was murky down in that corner and he couldn't see it. Maybe he should go to Specsavers or somewhere."

Harry Redknapp is irate at the assistant referee after QPR's 3-1 defeat to West Brom moved them to the bottom of the table

"As far as I'm concerned – I'm from Bristol and so is that lad – and he got it wrong."

Ian Holloway after referee Steve Dunn failed to award a foul for Man City's first goal

THE FUNNIEST QPR QUOTES... EVER!

OFF THE PITCH

"One of the lads said, 'Oh, I can remember the days when I used to buy my suits from Burton's' and I was thinking, 'Christ! I've got one at home I got from Asda!' I hadn't progressed as far as Burton's yet."

Ian Holloway on the culture shock when arriving as a player at QPR in the 1990/91 season

"I'm just disappointed my invite was lost in the post. I'm sure the Queen would have invited me, we got on so well the last time we met."

Neil Warnock on Prince William and Kate's royal wedding

"I stopped because I would be out drinking in the past and someone would come up to me outside a bar and call me a pr*ck or something. If I was drunk I would go for them and if I hit them they would go to the police. So I find it better just to stay away from it now."

Joey Barton remains out of trouble by avoiding nightlife

Landlord: "I've come looking for the rent."

Stan Bowles: "Well come on in and we can look for it together."

Bowles, who shared a flat with his QPR teammate Don Shanks, greets their landlord after gambling the rent money

"I need a bigger garden. I only had a little one. I told my wife after a week I was knackered. I tried to help by pulling out weeds and it turned out they were her plants! She wasn't very happy!"

Ian Holloway upsets the wife while on gardening leave at Rangers

"It wasn't the softest ground to dive on, but it was nice to get my Blue Peter badge – I can get into Alton Towers for half-price now!"

Chris Day focuses on the positives after appearing on Blue Peter as the goalie in their Superstars competition

"I'm not a young footballer any more. You grow up and see things in a very different way. I thought it was so wrong that I had a collection of designer watches worth hundreds of thousands. People are struggling to put food on the table and there I am with flash watches and cars. I told my PA to get rid of them. I can get a Casio watch for £6 which does the same job. I am about to sell my Aston Martin to buy a Prius."

Joey Barton feels guilty about his wealth

"Liverpool are my nap selection – I prefer to sleep when they're on the box."

Stan Bowles on Liverpool's style of football

"Where I'm from, if you couldn't defend yourself, you'd have your trainers nicked. If I went home crying that someone had hit me with their fists, I'd be told to pick up a stick, get back out and sort it."

Joey Barton on growing up as a kid in Liverpool

"That's how I get around – via betting shops. If I'm lost, I just think, 'Hang on, there's a bookies round here somewhere' and I soon find my bearings."

Stan Bowles doesn't need GPS navigation

"Chuffed to beans I made it through the three hours without fainting or crying. The pain was definitely worth it, pictures to follow."

Ian Holloway is given a tattoo by his son Will, who is a trained artist

"I'm a compulsive bird feeder. I hate to think of them going hungry. Bit mad, innit?"

Harry Redknapp spends £2,000 a year feeding birds

"I used to think you needed a passport to go south of Watford."

Neil Warnock's a true northerner

"My brother is really popular with the Canadians, he is their David Beckham. He was the only one singing the National Anthem – I think he learnt it off South Park."

Lee Bircham says his brother, and Canada international Marc, learned a lot from watching cartoons

"Sitting eating sushi in the city, incredibly chilled out reading Nietzsche."

Joey Barton tweets after signing for QPR

"I love animals so much, all animals. Apart from cats, I'm a little bit scared of cats."

Harry Redknapp stays away from felines

"I used to enjoy a drink with George Best. He was telling me one day about the statue of him they had put up in Belfast. I told him there was one of me outside Ladbrokes."

Stan Bowles on George Best

"If I hadn't been a footballer, I'd have been something else. For example, a priest. I mean, something different, something no one else does."

Rodney Marsh... OK then!

"My idea of relaxation? Going somewhere away from the wife."

Rangers skipper Terry Fenwick

"I mean no respect to Donatella [Versace]. I'm sure she would not be flattered to hear she looks like Marc Bircham."

Ian Holloway reckons his midfielder's hair makes him look like the fashion designer

"Olly started calling me Donatella because he gets so much stick from us for looking like Gollum, the goblin from the Lord of the Rings."

Bircham bites back

"How does Sven Goran Eriksson have the time to shag those birds of his? He's always at the football."

Stan Bowles on the England boss

"I was Labour until the Gordon Brown and Tony Blair debacle. Brown is a talentless idiot who I can't believe was running the country. It was left in a mess. I don't think the working class should be running the country and that's coming from me I am working class. I don't like Ed Miliband either. He is a d*ckhead. His voice is so strange its like a Monty Python scene where you see the other MPs sniggering behind his back."

Joey Barton talks politics

"If I am somewhere and there were four really ugly girls, I'm thinking, 'Well, she's not the worst'."

Barton describes UKIP as the best of a bad bunch of political parties

"I started talking to him about this game. I said, 'Bloody hell, we've scored some good goals'. I shouted to him, 'We've had a bloody great time, what about you?' His head's gone up and he was looking at me and you could see him thinking, 'What the f*ck are you talking about?'. I got too carried away in the end, went too close and he backed away and disappeared into the bracken. You couldn't tell he was there any more. He must have thought I was a right nutter."

Neil Warnock bumped into a stag during a bike ride around Richmond Park

"I will gladly go to jail for a month, in the name of free speech. I have no problem with what I said. Make me a martyr..."

Joey Barton versus the world

"I was invited to appear on the Kilroy show. The subject was gambling addicts. What it had to do with me, I'm not sure. I declined and spent the day at Sandown races."

QPR legend Stan Bowles

"I actually despise the whole of that firm, mentally deficient, turn up at the opening of an envelope, fame hungry, prized ball bags."

Joey Barton on the reality TV show TOWIE

"35 million [followers]?!? What the f*cking, f*ck! He looks little a shaved little bird with earrings. This is a truly f*cked up world, if he's 'cool'."

Joey Barton on Justin Bieber

"How can you call me a c*nt? You shagged your teammate's missus. You're the c*nt."

Anton Ferdinand to Chelsea's John Terry

"I think that clocking in to a factory would be the worst thing in the world. All you could say to the man next to you is, 'What's in your sandwich, Charlie?'"

Rodney Marsh, speaking with perspective in 1967

Q: "How much did you earn as a player, compared to Wayne Rooney?"

A: "Not enough to go to brothels."

Ian Holloway after Rooney admitted to having sex with prostitutes

"I think her mother loves me because we're a similar age."

Neil Warnock on his unlikely friendship with Delia Smith's mum

"I blew the lot on vodka and tonic, gambling and fags. Looking back, I think I overdid it on the tonic."

Stan Bowles has always loved a drink

THE FUNNIEST QPR QUOTES... EVER!

TALKING
BALLS

"I know everyone screams that he should play in the middle and I'm no nugget! I know what job he can do there."

Ian Holloway on playing Richard Langley in a central position

"I think it's his wallet – he isn't used to carrying that kind of money around so it's probably given him a hamstring strain!"

John Gregory on the injury suffered by Ray Jones, who had just signed a new contract

"He is a bit of a fruitcake but he's got amazing ability."

Harry Redknapp praises Adel Taarabt

"I wouldn't utter a word against Paulo Sousa. Then again, in three years with Rangers I think he was the seventh man in charge – or was it the eighth?"

QPR striker Dexter Blackstock – on loan at Forest – after Paulo Sousa was given the boot by Rangers

"I've got to be honest, you wouldn't want to have a fight with this fella. He's a big 'un.... I think we better give him an extra year on his contract in case he cops the needle with me."

Harry Redknapp on new signing Oguchi Onyewu

"Before the game, Naomi Campbell came into our dressing room and saw a few things."

Dexter Blackstock on the catwalk queen

"I said if he played well he could have a few days off. He is shooting off to catch a train. I think he is going to France, I can't tell with him. He is a rogue."

Neil Warnock on Adel Taarabt

"We had to bang a few heads together, which must have been the kick up the backside we needed."

Marc Bircham loves mixing metaphors

"What we've all got to do is pick him up, slap him around and make him feel welcome."

Ian Holloway helping the homesick Doudou

"He would run at fellas, looking at them and chatting to them while dribbling the ball between his heels."

Manager Alec Stock on Rodney Marsh

"Everyone calls him a gypsy but I can assure you he doesn't live in a caravan. He has a house with foundations."

Ian Holloway on his long-haired Argentine defender Gino Padula

"I'll probably have had enough of him by Christmas, so hopefully he'll score 10 or 15 goals by then and get himself a move."

Neil Warnock on managing Adel Taarabt

"Tommy Docherty was the worst manager I ever played under, though. Bestie once told me that if Docherty said it was raining, you should always check the weather before going outside. He came back to QPR in 1979 as manager and he said to me, 'You can trust me, Stan'. I told him I would rather trust my chickens with Colonel Sanders. He dropped me into the reserves for six months!"

Stan Bowles on his old boss

"I call him Ronseal, he does exactly what it says on the tin. He's an out-and-out winger. He can turn, he can beat people and he makes the right choice nearly every time."

Ian Holloway after on-loan Jerome Thomas netted the winner for QPR at Swindon

"Barcelona want him? Maybe we'll do a straight swap with Messi."

Harry Redknapp is happy to let go of Adel Taarabt

"[George Santos] is a big lad. He can clean out your guttering without standing on a ladder."

Ian Holloway marvels at his player's height

"Paul Furlong is my vintage Rolls Royce and he cost me nothing. We polish him, look after him and I have him fine-tuned by my mechanics. We take good care of him because we have to drive him every day, not just save him for weddings."

Ian Holloway wants to keep his veteran forward motoring

"My lot are the ugliest team ever to have worn the blue and white hoops – we certainly don't sell many calendars. In my playing days we had some right good looking b*ggers. But this lot are the worst I have ever seen. They all look like dogs."

Holloway doesn't fancy his QPR his players

"I just thought he was a disgrace. I will fine him as much as I possibly can. I told him to his face, 'You've let me down and you've let the team down'."

Neil Warnock after Armand Traore's red card

"Mr [Gordon] Jago, I'd like to say on behalf of the lads: We're 40 per cent behind you."

Rodney Marsh welcomes the new manager

"Gareth Ainsworth is the most physical winger I've seen. He calls himself the wolf man because of his sideburns but I don't pick fault with hairdos if players perform."

Ian Holloway praises his midfielder's hair

"He has no responsibility whatsoever. The players aren't allowed to pass to him in our half. I told them that. I decided pre-season. He's liable to do something we haven't thought about."

Neil Warnock on how he controls Adel Taarabt

"When my wife first saw Marc for the first time, she said he was a fine specimen of a man. She says I have nothing to worry about, but I think she wants me to buy her a QPR shirt with his name on the back for Christmas."

Is Ian Holloway a little threatened by striker Marc Nygaard?

"He's the quickest thing we've got, and an absolute animal."

Ian Holloway admires Danny Shittu's speed

"The funniest thing was at the end of the game Shaun Derry didn't even realise we were down to 10 men."

Nedum Onuoha says his teammate had somehow missed Adel Taarabt's red card

"The world is full of nutters who are going to send you messages slagging you off."

Harry Redknapp after Chris Samba received abuse for his display against Fulham

"Our new Czech keeper Jan Stejskal only knows three words of English – 'my ball', 'away' and one other."

Ray Wilkins loses count

"The doctor grafted a bit of Danny's hamstring onto his knee, but that won't be a problem for him. He's got more hamstring than the rest of the squad put together."

Ian Holloway appreciates Shittu's thighs

"My wife said I looked good in hoops. After QPR there weren't that many options."

Marc Bircham on joining Yeovil, who wear green and white hoops

"He played in a reserve team game the other day, and I could have run about more than he did."

Harry Redknapp criticises Adel Taarabt after defeat to Liverpool

"He's been out for a year and Richard Langley is still six months away from being Richard Langley, and I could do with a fully fit Richard Langley."

Ian Holloway on his Hoops midfielder

"You need someone to grab people by the throat – in a nice way – and get them going."

Neil Warnock after signing Joey Barton

A FUNNY
OLD GAME

"[Eden] Hazard's only crime is he hasn't kicked him hard enough."

Joey Barton backs the Chelsea player who lashed out on a Swansea ballboy when he laid on a ball to waste time

"I can think of a lot of players who would have kicked a bit harder than he did."

Harry Redknapp also defends Hazard after he was shown a red for kicking the ballboy

"Before my Besiktas debut, they sacrificed a lamb on the pitch and daubed its blood on my forehead for luck. They never did that at QPR."

Les Ferdinand on the culture differences

"Sitting here scratching my head how Pastore and Lucas Moura start before Lavezzi? I know Pastore scored but he is terrible. Pastore wouldn't get a beach ball off me if we where locked in a phone box. He's turd. Anyone who thinks he isn't is clueless."

Joey Barton attacks PSG's Javier Pastore

"I rung Kenny Jacket straight away to congratulate him on getting Swansea promoted and he said, 'I'm waiting to get my goalie out of jail'. You can't even celebrate these days, can you?"

Ian Holloway on the pitfalls of celebrating. Swansea's Willy Gueret was arrested at the end of their promotion-winning game at Bury

"I tell you another crazy, crazy, crazy rule. We want women to come to football don't we? I think they're bloody pretty – a damn sight prettier than any bloke I've seen. You talk to women about footballers and what do they like – they like legs and our shorts are getting longer. We should go back to the days when half your a*se was hanging out. Why can't you let players lift up their shirts? Who is it disrespecting? What's wrong with letting a load of young ladies see a good-looking lad take his shirt off? They'd have to watch other teams, though – because my team is as ugly as hell."

Ian Holloway talks about football shorts

"Sir Geoff Hurst and Martin Peters were always together. Boring as f*ck they were, would send you to sleep."

Stan Bowles on the 1966 World Cup winners

"Everyone loves Alex Ferguson and he's a great, great manager, but he couldn't put on a coaching session to save his life. I've spoken to people about it – he can barely lay out cones."

Joey Barton on the legendary manager

"I wouldn't trust the FA to show me a good manager if their lives depended on it."

Harry Redknapp is not a fan

"There's a Burton's 10 minutes from where we live. She probably thought it was there."
Harry Redknapp on reports he didn't get the England job because his wife didn't want to live near St George's Park National Football Centre, in Burton-upon-Trent

"Brazil just aren't that Brazilian any more. Like Harlem Globetrotters just travelling round for the dough."
Joey Barton after Brazil drew with Russia

"Wayne Rooney may have a weight problem. His head must weigh three stone."
Stan Bowles has his say on the striker

"No monetary bullshit. No media b*llocks. Just pure, old school, mortgages and livelihoods on the line, balls-out football. I feel that training in the lower leagues will give me a reality check and maybe help me become a better person; a little more humility will serve me well."

Joey Barton training with Fleetwood Town before a potential loan deal collapsed

"People are going on like he's actually eaten someone. Nobody has died. Worse things happen in nurseries every day of the week. Move on FFS!"

Joey Barton on the Luis Suarez biting incident

"My arms withered and my body was covered with puss-like sores, but no matter how bad it got, I consoled myself by remembering that I wasn't a Chelsea fan."
Ian Holloway on QPR's local rivals

"Can someone take the helium of Carragher for the after-the-match stuff. Dogs all over England standing to attention every time he speaks..."
Joey Barton pokes fun at the TV pundit

"I used to trip myself up in the penalty area. Rodney Marsh showed me how to do it."
Where Stan Bowles got his tricks from

"Everyone had a rattle and they went just to enjoy the game. If that sounds a rose-tinted or nostalgic memory, I'm sorry, but it's true. Then, for me, and my dad, it was a cheese roll at a little cafe up the road, the 106 bus and then the 227 back to Polar."

Harry Redknapp on his boyhood trips to watch West Ham play

"Hopefully they stop trying to be an Orwellian organisation and get to grips with the change that's happening in the world around them. Don't understand how they can try to police a technology they understand very little about."

Joey Barton hits out against the FA after he received a warning letter over a tweet

"Neymar is the Justin Bieber of football. Brilliant on the old YouTube. Cat p*ss in reality. Stop going on about goals in Brazil Lge as well. I once scored 77 in 1 season in the Rainhill and Byrne U14 league and that's a stronger comp."

Joey Barton takes a swipe at the Brazil star

"Football supporters don't care what you do as long as you're a good footballer. They would sing Saddam Hussein's name if he scored a few goals for their team."

Harry Redknapp on the fickle nature of fans

"He's a mercenary. You can't really back him. Sure, I'm a hoodlum, I've got into scrapes – but Tevez is someone who in the last six months has gone on strike, gone off to Argentina to play golf, tried to get himself sacked. If that's not the epitome of what's wrong with modern players, I don't know what is."

Joey Barton slams midfielder Carlos Tevez

"Look at the prickly little fella down the road at Chelsea. He wants to win everything and we can learn from that. If there were two flies crawling up the wall he'd be desperate to back the winner."

Ian Holloway on Jose Mourinho

HOOPS A DAISY

"I call us the orange club – because our future's bright!"

Ian Holloway has high hopes for QPR

"I thought QPR were a Scottish club, but I said to myself, 'Why not, if it's good for them and me?'

Stephane Mbia after joining from Marseille

"So we walked into the Lancaster Gate Hotel the night before – and in the foyer were these Swedish birds with dresses up to their bums."

Frank Sibley recalls the evening before QPR won the League Cup in 1967

"If the club was a chocolate bar, it would have licked itself."

Ian Holloway on QPR's time in the top flight

"It's easier to stick to 'sir' or 'gaffer' on the training ground than to try to remember their names."

Mikele Leigertwood on the many QPR bosses

"Over the years, QPR have been a bit of a flitty, farty, we-like-a-fancy-Dan-footballer club."

Ian Holloway wants more grounded players

"This is our cave, and I like living in it."

Ian Holloway on remaining at Loftus Road

91

"When my mum was running our house, when I was a kid, all the money was put into tins. She knew what was in every tin and I know how much I've got in my tin – that's the way we'll run this club."

Ian Holloway won't spend money that Rangers don't have

"If we did get promoted there would be a tear in my eye and my wife would hammer me. I didn't cry at my wedding or the birth of my children and she has warned me not to cry or I'll be in trouble."

Marc Bircham before QPR lost to Cardiff in the play-off final

"QPR is the people's club and everybody can have a piece of that pie. A pie that's already smelling beautifully."

Ian Holloway likes a pie

"One or two bad eggs have spoiled it. If it had been done my way, they would have been out of the building straight away."

Joey Barton blasts his teammates over QPR's relegation campaign

"The club isn't on solid ground. It's like I'm on a block of ice. I don't know whether I'm going through it, or slide off."

Ian Holloway on coming into QPR

"It's been embarrassing, he's won every award. He won Groundsman of the Year and Young Player of the Year – even at the age of 37!"

Ian Holloway on Paul Furlong winning all the club's end-of-season honours

"QPR is my team now. The grandkids are all getting QPR kit this week."

Harry Redknapp forcing Christmas presents on his family members

"When QPR seemed to be dying, we were a carcass and the vultures came and fed off our bones."

Ian Holloway on having to sell his players

"I can't believe QPR have just been relegated and Bosingwa was walking down the tunnel laughing.... Embarrassing. Show some guts man... The League table doesn't lie. Both sides haven't won enough games to deserve to stay up. Reading in a better position than QPR though. Gutted for the club. To many w*nkers amongst the playing staff. All brought in by [former manager Mark] Hughes. Some good lads but not enough. Too many maggots. Hope they can get a load out, if not they'll end up in a Wolves situation because trust me that Championship is a f*cking hard league!"

Joey Barton blasts Jose Bosingwa after he was caught laughing following QPR's relegation

THE FUNNIEST QPR QUOTES... EVER!

BEST OF ENEMIES

"Accept you failed. Accept you're to blame. Be humble and apologise to a club you left in a hell of a worse situation than when you came."

Joey Barton to Mark Hughes after relegation

"He [Taarabt] is not injured. He's not fit. He's not fit to play football unfortunately. He played in a reserve game the other day and I could have run about more than he did. I can't pick him. I can't keep protecting people who don't want to run about and train, who are about three stone overweight. What am I supposed to keep saying, keep getting your 60, 70 grand a week but don't train? What's the game coming to?"

Harry Redknapp attacks Adel Taarabt after his side was beaten 3-2 by Liverpool

"The only reason he has lost weight is because he has had tonsillitis, that's the only way we could get any weight off of him. He is not fit to play a game, that's the truth. He is the worst professional I have ever come across and I have been his only ally at QPR for the past three years."

Harry Redknapp after Adel Taarabt had slimmed down

"He spends most of the time in his office but when he gets off the phone he comes down to watch for five or 10 minutes – he never takes a session."

Adel Taarabt responds to Harry Redknapp

"For many years I have thought he was the gutter type – I was going to call him a sewer rat, but that might be insulting to sewer rats. He's the lowest of the low and I can't see him being at Blackburn much longer."

Neil Warnock blasts Blackburn's El-Hadji Diouf after he abused Jamie Mackie as he lay on the floor with a broken leg

"You horrible disgusting man E H Diouf! Your time will come!"

Bradley Orr tweets his reaction to Diouf

"That **** Diouf will get it one day, what goes around comes around."

Paddy Kenny also weighs in

"That c*** will get what's coming to him."

Clint Hill has his say on Diouf

"Lost his job and the guy is blaming everyone but himself! Embarrassing, time to look in the mirror mate. Last thing we need right now."

"Not a big fan of people that try to make scape-goats out of others. If u live by the sword, u die by it. If I talked about Neil, he'd do well to get another job. Twitter cost him his job???? I can think of a million other things! #shutitwarnock

"Neil Warnock saying I talk to much. Now that is funny #mikebassett,"

Joey Barton's tweets on Neil Warnock

THE FUNNIEST QPR QUOTES... EVER!

"Love twitter. Where else could you debate politics with a woman-beating scumbag. #peopleinglasshouses."

Karl Henry gets in a Twitter spat with Stan Collymore

"@StanCollymore This is why nobody wants you on TV. If you're going to give it, take it!! Stop crying FFS! I've heard enough!!"

Henry continues to smack Collymore

"Get ya mum in, plays the field well son! #sket."

Rio Ferdinand insults the mother of a Twitter user who said, "Maybe QPR will sign a good CB they need one."

"Come and have a chat big man. When u feel like talking to me face to face just come. monday tuesday thirsday [sic] or Friday."
Djibril Cisse responds to a fan who said he "couldn't hit a cow's a*se with a banjo" with the address of the club's training ground

"I've seen Boris Johnson from Norwich with his sign at the darts. He's irrelevant really, absolute no mark."
Joey Barton after Norwich's Bradley Johnson held a placard during the world darts final at Alexandra Palace, which said: "Barton your breath stinks"

THE FUNNIEST QPR QUOTES... EVER!

"Shearers still on my case... I know I f*cked up Alan, thanks for stating the obvious. Whilst we're both stating the obvious about each other, can I just say for the record what a great player u were. Well better than me...

"But I have a better hair (which is not hard), wear well better shirts on TV and have a personality (something u lack).

"I really don't like that pr*ck, in fact I honestly despise him... I'd take it off Hansen and Gary Lineker but not from that bell, same fella that stamped on Neil Lennon, then threatened FA if they banned him that he would retire from international football.

"No sorry, not having him, never have. Selfish, boring man him. He can do one. My favourite memory of him though is when he dropped his spuds when Keano put it on him. Goodnight Al, sleep well matey…"

Joey Barton's series of tweets after Alan Shearer criticised his meltdown at Man City

"'Do u wanna go there publicly 'Mr Squeaky Clean'? Think u should have a look in that vast closet of skeletons before u respond.

"I know a lot about THAT side to u the people don't and won't bat an eye lid at exposing u. So mind ur manners Squeaky… now back under your stone you odious little toad…"

Barton after Gary Lineker defended Shearer

THE FUNNIEST QPR QUOTES... EVER!

CALL THE MANAGER

"I don't pay Danny Shittu to pass the ball. I don't pay him to be pretty, I pay him to defend and be in the right place because he's a big monster. Him and Clarke Carlisle have got to sort their lives out and defend for us."

Ian Holloway takes a swipe at his defensive pairing

"We defended like fairies in the first half but the first two goals could have come straight out of the Premier League."

BBC Match of the Day bosses ruled Warnock's "fairies" comment was "unacceptable" after a viewer complained

"We're like a bad teabag – we never stay in the cup that long."

Ian Holloway after QPR's Carling Cup defeat by Aston Villa

"We need a big, ugly defender. If we had one of them we'd have dealt with County's first goal by taking out the ball, the player and the first three rows of seats in the stands."

Ian Holloway after QPR's encounter with Notts County

"I reckon the ball was travelling at 400mph and I bet it burned the keeper's eyebrows off."

Ian Holloway's view away at Crewe

"It was tense and I was dying for the toilet. As soon as Kevin [McLeod] scored, I went."
Ian Holloway dashed to the bogs after the midfielder's 88th-minute goal in QPR's 2-0 win over Wrexham

"Richard Langley looked like he was still in Trinidad and Tobago playing for Jamaica. He's got to realise what it's all about. It's not just him, it's all of them, but I'll start with the big ones and work my way down, because that ain't good enough."
Ian Holloway after QPR are shocked by non-league side Vauxhall Motors in an FA Cup replay

110

"I lost to Vauxhall Motors in the cup on penalties – now you don't get much more embarrassing than that because their name is atrocious isn't it? It sounded like we were beaten by a car. We didn't get into first gear and were automatically knocked out of the cup. It meant that much that a taxi driver who is now a good friend of mine came in and spoke to me for two hours about what I should have done. But then I looked at the team he would have picked and I said, 'They're all bloody injured, you complete pillock'. He didn't realise how hard it was being a football manager."

Ian Holloway later recalls the time Second Division QPR were knocked out of the cup by the minnows

"Whoever that was, I would like to pull his pants down and slap his a*se like I used to do to my kids. Apparently I'm not even allowed to do that anymore otherwise I will have the old health and safety on my back giving it the old 'hello'. The world's gone mad. Tony Blair won the election, so why's he gotta resign? I think the Conservative fella should. If he couldn't win an election with a failing government, or a flailing government, what's the matter with him? Get out you ain't no good. I know we're not talking football... we are aren't we?"

Ian Holloway responds to a journalist who claimed Danny Shittu was being sold

"We looked more like Queens Park Strangers out there."

Ian Holloway after five players made their debuts for QPR against Leeds

"He won't talk to me on Twitter, as I don't know what Twitter is."

Harry Redknapp on QPR transfer target Peter Odemwingie

"Once we had got the equaliser I wanted to put jump leads on my players because I thought we had an excellent chance of nicking a win."

Ian Holloway on a missed opportunity after QPR's draw at Forest

"Do you believe everything you read in The Sun? They've got some nice tits in that paper."
When Ian Holloway was asked about reports linking him with the vacant Millwall job

"I think it is these stupid boots, they're like carpet slippers. Don't talk to me about these boots."
Neil Warnock after DJ Campbell got injured in training

"There was a spell in the second half when I took my heart off my sleeve and put it in my mouth."
Ian Holloway after Rangers beat Coventry

"One of their members of staff has been as rude as f*ck about us, so it's about us coming out on top. It's not about pretty football, it's about winning football. We've got to go out today. Let's get on our f*cking toes. Let's get in here. All my life I've been on a crusade because you can be a winner without being rude. Get f*cking focused. Get in nice and tight. Feel that f*cking strength."

Ian Holloway's pep talk to his players ahead of a win over Brighton

"You say cheats don't prosper but I think in this case he has done."

Neil Warnock blames Bradley Johnson for Barton's red card

"If is a big word. If I had long hair I could be a rock star."

Ian Holloway responding to a reporter who asked if striker Tony Thorpe had put away a good opportunity at Bristol City

"Every time Ipswich crossed into our box I felt I might have to go through a new pair of strides."

Ian Holloway after QPR's 2-2 draw away

"There was an incident in the second half, when Bobby Zamora dived to get West Ham a free-kick. That was a real splash."

Ian Holloway on the West Ham striker apparently diving

"The first goal, one header from a header and the kid's through on goal. It's Raggy A*se Rovers. For the second one, when have you seen Clint Hill mess about like that? He thought he was Jose Enrique or someone."

Neil Warnock fumes at Clint Hill against Millwall

"Well a few of them have had their hair done."

Ian Holloway on how the TV cameras affected his players

"[Richard Langley] over-elaborated with his celebration. He looked like a chicken stick."

Ian Holloway on Langley's goal celebration

"I am disappointed in the way we lost, it could have been double figures in the end as Paddy Kenny was fantastic, I thought, to keep it respectable."

Neil Warnock says Watford could have beaten QPR by 10 goals

"I was up and down like Zebedee from the Magic Roundabout. We had a monster team out there, all the big guys, the roof inspectors as I call them."

Ian Holloway after QPR came back from two down to beat Leicester 3-2

"After the game, we're walking off the pitch. We've just won 2-1. The ref's given us a goal that was blatantly offside, so I'm absolutely elated. Neil Warnock, the Sheffield United manager, is going ballistic. Anyhow, I am shouting at Neil, as we walk off, 'I always supported you. But now I see I was wrong. Everybody else in football is right. You are a tw*t'."

Ian Holloway on Neil Warnock

"The fat lady hasn't started to sing yet, but she has a mic in her hand."

Ian Holloway concedes QPR's chances of reaching the play-offs are virtually over

"You say [they are] talented players but are they that talented? I don't know really. They won't go. How are you going to get rid of them? That's your biggest problem. They all have contracts. I wish you were right, and you could say [the players would leave] but it ain't going to happen here. How are they going to go? Who is going to pay them what they are earning here? It is going to be very hard to shift them. It is not a case of players wanting to leave suddenly. I hear that all the time that if they get relegated they want to go because they don't want to play in the Championship, but if they f*cking played better, then they would not be in the Championship so that's a load of cobblers."

Redknapp after a defeat at Everton leaves QPR 10 points off safety with five games left

"We were like the Dog and Duck in the first half and Real Madrid in the second. We can't go on like that. At full time I was at them like an irritated Jack Russell."

Ian Holloway after QPR came back from two goals down to draw with Hull

"I am not happy we lost 4-0, but sometimes you have to smile through adversity."

Neil Warnock in philosophical mood after a defeat by Bolton

"I couldn't be more chuffed if I were a badger at the start of the mating season."

Ian Holloway is thrilled after QPR beat Cardiff

"I was disappointed with our fans and with their fans. I'd like to say to ours, 'You should have stayed'. Everybody who did stay, well done, you deserved that. Don't go home early. You might not have missed your last bus, but you missed a treat... And as for their fans, 'Getting sacked in the morning?' I don't think so."

Ian Holloway blasts both sets of fans after QPR netted two stoppage-time goals to snatch a 2-2 draw at home to Brentford

"In comparison to Frank Lampard, it is like taking a baby for a walk. It is ridiculous."

Neil Warnock likens Frank Lampard's strong challenge at Wolves to other tackles that ended up with red cards

"It was funny. It was quite strange to hear Joey trying to talk in a French accent, that is for sure. But I don't really know Joey and he is out on loan from QPR, so I am hoping he keeps learning French."

Harry Redknapp reacts to Joey Barton speaking with a French twang at a Marseille press conference where he is on loan

"It's one of my proudest days in football, but I've caught the bouquet again. I'm always the bridesmaid."

Ian Holloway after QPR were defeated in the play-off final

THE FUNNIEST QPR QUOTES... EVER!

SAY THAT AGAIN?

"To put it in gentleman's terms if you've been out for a night and you're looking for a young lady and you pull one, some weeks they're good looking and some weeks they're not the best. Our performance today would have been not the best looking bird but at least we got her in the taxi. She weren't the best looking lady we ended up taking home but she was very pleasant and very nice, so thanks very much, let's have a coffee."

Ian Holloway's most famous post-match comments after a win against Chesterfield

"If you can't score, you can't win."

Paulo Sousa is learning the rules fast

"We've picked the ship up off the bottom of the ocean, plugged a few leaks and we're floating on the top. Now we want to turn around and sail off into the sunset."

Ian Holloway on QPR's achievements over the season

"You never count your chickens before they hatch. I used to keep parakeets and I never counted every egg thinking I would get all eight birds. You just hoped they came out of the nest box looking all right."

Ian Holloway when asked if QPR can get automatically promoted

"You can say that strikers are a bit like postmen, they have to get in and out as quick as they can before the dog has a go."

Ian Holloway on his forwards

"When the chips are down, the top dogs usually come up smelling of roses."

Neil Warnock loves his cliches after QPR's unbeaten start to the season

"When you play with wingers you look a bit like a taxi with both doors open, anyone can get in or out."

Ian Holloway is not happy with a pre-season friendly result

Say That Again?

"Every dog has its day – and today is woof day! Today I just want to bark."

Ian Holloway on the promotion-winning victory at Sheffield Wednesday

"I want you to bad rash them."

Ian Holloway during his pre-match team talk on BBC Radio 5 Live

"We're 5-0 down with a minute to go on this one."

Ian Holloway on trying to sign Middlesbrough midfielder Andrew Davies who apparently wanted more money

"I'm like a swan at the moment. I look fine on top of the water but under the water my little legs are going mad."

Ian Holloway after QPR beat Bristol City

"Right now, everything is going wrong for me – if I fell in a barrel of boobs, I'd come out sucking my thumb!"

Ian Holloway bemoans his bad luck

"When the water stands still in the pond, it starts to stink."

Ian Holloway on dropping players

Say That Again?

"It's like putting a snake in a bag, if you don't tie it up, it will wriggle free."

Ian Holloway hails the spirit of his players after they rescued a point against Millwall

"[Loic] Remy looked like he might be getting over that groin strain. He showed a few flashes."

Harry Redknapp in full Carry On mode

"Now I'm a little fella as it happens, but when I was really small I was nothing."

Ian Holloway on being picked up by Bristol Rovers as a kid

"Who would have thought a few weeks ago that we would be sitting in this position now? It's like the song, 'Wait a minute, it stopped hailing, guys are swimming, gals are sailing'. I love that song."

Ian Holloway on QPR being in the top half of the table

"It's like the film Men in Black. I walk around in a black suit, white shirt and black tie where I've had to flash my white light every now and again to erase some memories, but I feel we've got hold of the galaxy now. It's in our hands."

Ian Holloway on coping with QPR's financial constraints

"I always say that scoring goals is like driving a car. When the striker is going for goal, he's pushing down that accelerator, so the rest of the team has to come off that clutch. If the clutch and the accelerator are down at the same time, then you are going to have an accident."

Ian Holloway on his strike force

"If you can keep your noses in front at the end, that's what counts. It's been said that I have a bit of a Roman nose and I am keeping it ahead at the moment. Hopefully it's all about the length of your hooter because I might be in front at the end of the season as well!"

Ian Holloway after QPR's win over Brighton

Printed in Great Britain
by Amazon

34192573R00078